Gary Lobo
419 - 329 - 2166

ENRIDGED

Selected Pieces
2000-2010

Brian Richards

 **PRESS**

Printed in the United States of America

Brian Richards

ENRIDGED

Selected Pieces 2000-2010

ISBN: 978-1-60801-047-9

Library of Congress Control Number: 1608010163

Copyright © 2011 by UNO Press

All rights reserved.

uoPRESS

University of New Orleans Press

unopress.org

Managing Editor: Bill Lavender

Book Design: Carrie Chappell

Thanks to Ken Warren for including a number of these poems in *House Organ.*

Thanks to Dawn Richards for the front and back cover photographs.

ENRIDGED

For Lily, Amanda, Kate, and Zoe

Tall daughters
are easy

on the old
man's back

The pertinent Spanish word is *desdén*—that's when you turn your back on the bull.

–Ed Dorn

The ridge is serpentine curves in every direction going one direction. It rises at the confluence of Rocky Fork and the south branch of Scioto Brush in western Scioto County and swells south as Bracken Ridge, bound on the west by Blue Creek, toward which it sends several substantial spurs, and on its steeper, unroadworthy eastern slope by Rocky. Bracken runs a few points west of south and becomes Mount Unger Ridge after the first large western spur runs out to Wamsley and the confluence of Turkey Creek from the west and Blue Creek from the south that forms the south fork of Scioto Brush. Mount Unger continues south to a second western spur, Silver Ridge, where Bro Richard's house sits, where SR125 winds up from Rocky into Adams County to run Silver down to the village of Blue Creek, and where the main ridge loses its name and veers for several miles just east of south back into Scioto County before turning abruptly and finally west. It throws a spur southeast to buttress its turn, a swell almost level, at 1300 feet the highest point in the ridge, over 800 feet above the Ohio, five miles south to the crow. At the end of the peak, surrounded by the headwaters of Upper Twin: the shanty. Where the ridge turns west, it reenters Adams County and forms the boundary between Green and Jefferson townships. The waters of Green flow south to the Ohio; Jefferson carries the Blue Creek watershed north to Scioto Brush on its way east to the Scioto River, then south to the Ohio and west to join the rain that fell a few feet away fifty miles back. About a mile after its western turn, the ridge dips to the gap between Upper Twin and Churn Creek, the eastern head of Blue Creek. As it rises back to level, it becomes Sunshine Ridge and immediately throws the long spur of Buckhorn Ridge south to the river, dividing the Upper and Lower Twin Creeks, forming the State Wilderness Area. The last hollow on Bloody Upper Twin before it reaches the flood plain of the Ohio is Tucker's Run, seat of the family compound, the incunabula of the twice and future press, home of Houndog. Sunshine snakes west around the enormous hollows of Silver Mine and DeMazie that head Lower Twin, dropping Carter's Run, Slate Fork, and Johnson's Run north to Churn Creek, spurring Blackburn Ridge out to the river between Lower Twin and Long Lick, and another between Long Lick and the Southdown fork of Stout's Run before dropping down to the gap at Rome Hill, from which vantage in winter the glint of the Ohio may be seen miles away down Stout's Run. On the north side of the gap lie the middle fork of Blue Creek and the yellow cottage where Bloody Twin Press offered its first corporeal manifestations, then the ridge levels again as Mount Tabor, outriggers north above Riley Hollow and south above Puntenney and Green to the gap between the West Fork of Stout's Run and the south of Mill Creek, the west fork of Blue. From there its last rise spreads mesa-like to confront the valley of Ohio Brush, where its sandstone bed is finally revealed in the cliffs of Buzzard's Roost.

Henceforth resisting if not
the swarms that dance between
the eye and the page turning barely
visible dots that run the skin and streak
thin red when wiped then iced
amber of which there is considerable
more than time and energy to load
her and sing it so
                    the dangers are temples
turned domestic exiled to build higher only
the bed comfortable everything hewn without
electric or running water, that he might not attract some
earthly consort and earn her disdain

The hornets work ceaselessly little
gunships blunder among
the flies until they strike too
quick to see turning it in their mouths
wings fluttering to the floor.

Rustle of Mme Towhee raking in the dough (cf

                                                  duff

dries fast on the ridge and the next rain springs it
up to flock the sides of everything stationary a tide
line that measures the velocity of each drop as winks
a desiccated piece of leaf or limb into the falling
air plasters it onto whatever available
surface to just that height thus certified

Ten feet up from thirteen
hundred asl in the aether holding
her sun below them as breasts the lower
ridge, her hair, skin, the oaks revealed in
light reflected from the pale
earthside of the leaves
                    then idle
down the lane somnambulescent greens
the miles down Mackletree past Boobie's mill and remuda,
Jonas' peacocks and the lost house where Zoe was born to
the lake and Turkey Creek, sun high, corn and beans drying
by the minute, over the penultimate hump to the valley and
it's not there
                    at about six hundred it's
brilliant and blank but he drives doubtless into knowing
the river has risen a hundred feet in
the night though the additional footage is thin
enough to breathe

Plump passiform too high in
a hickory to identify; towhees
scratching in the leaves, sun
a rosy memory above the ridge, white-throated
sparrow, first this fall, Peabody here.

The chestnut oaks hold sometimes
bewitched faeries beseeched arms up
away from a later fallen
killed by its tears
plumb rocket to the roof
cymbal squared by the foot.

We release them as they lie to us
unable to be what they were despite
we are looking at them in situ.

It would serve us if they came
back from the celluloid
and we had to live again with all the created
struck Olympian in flesh by wood and feather.

Tree frogs and crickets for the first time in
weeks, bugs out, long-eared owl
A hundred feet NE tires round the bend at
Mackletree audible before the motor which throb then
commands the ear until it drops over the gap and below
the threshold. Listening for her downshift, the sweep of her
light through the trees below.

The trees are still full in their shift to the upper
end of the spectrum, hurtling away. The ground is
littered, the sun leaks in, humidity out, the cars going
through the gap 200 feet below seem closer
already a comfort going by.

Awning windows fill the S & E walls at the head of the bed open and loaded with light direct and original, as are the odd varieties in the stories and between them. The slope falls gently at first south, chestnut oak limbs revealed and supplicant but neighbored by siblings whose leaves stay ochre and sere, among the red oaks leafed in dried blood and red oaks naked sun piling through. Down the steep slope to the north, green oaks, red and chestnut, visible since the hickories outside the east window have lost every leaf. The understory is still vibrant with small maples, verdant or gone to yellow, gold, red among the sassafras whose soft and downy leaves have wiped his ass for the last six months but are harder to find now in the morning light, though still good through gold. Weeks of mild leaves floating down one at a time or cascades in a sudden gust slipping along the metal roof as Motian's brushes behind Evans measure the conjunction: the ridge in daily tune.

Ruby's on the ridge
                    round
midnight the enormous sky in a ten-acre field highest spot for miles but vague
light everywhere on the horizon

          sisters still
bright above

Seven p.m. and the sun dropped behind Buckhorn
Ridge to the SW the crepuscular array (novel after all
those years in the hollor the ridge west right outside
the window then this summer with its baffling
canopy) balancing nicely the passing front that gouaches
a line ten degrees above the eastern ridge
                                        below
that, gloom, while the west completes it
's spectral decline to the tear that winks ultra

In the south a river of blue just over
the Ohio, Houndog in the evening
sun though it is dark on Tucker and the day
is dying and, O Egypt, did you ever
have a mind to make up?

Tomorrow the moon   but tonight
just past full   the head
a little off   nimbled with cloud
top   "stippled
with want"

                winds pushing
thirty swaying oak
tops in concentric patterns backlit
periodically by the moon through
the heavy scrub   tree just fell
near the pick up   no
sound of glass   limber oaks

She loves to
play

his bass
upright ain't

the word
the way

it sounds

Giving the birds
his ear song swollen with
desire the woods disturbed by scant demands
craving the untended as
intended
              with us the provocative twitter
& chirp of tyrant love this far
from cats & pesticides, secure in
bug-rich shade, cycling in spate.

Line tied eight feet up between
a young hickory and a younger red maple to hold
the outdoor shower system—five gal black vinyl
sack and dependent nozzle—holds also a nuthatch
walking upside down a trick for the prospective
missus who watches as she walks down
the hickory then zips off as he flies
toward her in pursuit as hot
as she is.

Psapfos in
mid may must be
the season of

which is why
she goes in
the first place

and comes back in
any case not
the second

Full moon can't sleep wanna do it
blues. Whippoorwill's sharp initial note drops
a third before the barked third time
after time, a dozen dozen ere it ends, that bark that
supplies the air or stores enough to go on

April on Friday the redbud weren't
there Saturday the clearcut just west of the divide on 125
revealed understory beyond his eyes' ability to make
sense of that much lavender on a hillside coming around
Plummer Fork on fire then four
inches of snow at the house though none on
Mackletree lavender and white slipping down
Plummer this morning past the burn
white on black

Predicate: what any preface predicts you could
say you'd be right if you said that but
you'd only know that
whatever that would be would be
said post nominally. Later
says you
from the head.

Waited until midnight without
fret, without bass, through the rain—might
she stay in town and avoid the slippery assent?—in bed
with a late *Sulfur* when the lights came up
the drive and she thumped through the door all
noise and light, up the ladder, onto the bed and on
to him
                    as though they could part time
be more than a portion separate and walk through into
thrushes and baffled light
a set of monodies like
library breasts high on her
chest canopied as though the gut
unclenched and she flew
in him
                    four times
the horn blew up
the holler
damped again by a quarter
mile of rustled leaves sometimes covered
with whippoorwill and chat

                              click

                                        descending

pair
            trill

Yellow-headed, wing-barred warbler working
the cohosh and maple sprouts in the drizzle. Bird song
constant through the day: chats, warblers, nuthatches
sparrows, robins, thrushes, the occasional
cardinal. Wren looking through
the slider, phoebes busy in
the nest under the eave: clucking, thin
peeps, scurry of wings.

In betrayal lies   But it's better
freedom. Who is   than being
untrusted is made
responsible thereby.   bitter about it

    Desmond: I wanted to sound like a dry
        martini.

One on   one on Sunday
Sunday morning   morning
                that
Sunday morning. Blue winged warblers, ready to dance.

Ridged Oaks

They are harps as Shelley wished
himself and more
                    than any save Sappho
seemed. Point loaded, bass unseen but
spread a
            like distance twined top and bottom. No
rise runs plumb but twists with wind
sun and the unspared
                        rod. Near the top
each trunk divides and reaps a surface
quotient to the light as catches
coincidentally the breeze, however
slight. It is
            they that susurrate the earth
's incessant eastward roll, a surface furze unheard from
the plane that takes some one else somewhere
                                        else. Or
whine and shatter, torqued by the articulative
wind that moans their chords below.

Lipspil

The descent of the tetons	over basin& range of rib	sinuous slip of belly	into the nest of her lips
over basin& range of ribs	that swell to hold	in vibrant air	her lungs release the song
sinuous slip of belly	in vibrant air	fibrillates the down	that models its sine
into the nest of her lips	her lungs release the song	that models its sine	along her come cry

Genetic diversity
preserves the inessential, why
some women have dark aureoles that cover a conic
projection while others nothing but a pale
vestige on which a button of like color
sits. Evolution teaches both are suitable
for suckling, but what prepared us for the cornucopia of
tits wherever we turn, the net wracked with popping
cookies lecturing to the barely contained and how could
one variety be preferred to the point that the others
remain unreproduced? America may be
the threatened land as promised wherein such variety is
homogenized so all nipples become moderate in size,
medial in shade, and immediately in sight. They will surely
still nourish if sucked. Or seen. The quality
of sustenance is not strained though it save us every day.

How can people who call a team
representing LA the Lakers be
expected to understand that
deregulation means things are
not, by definition, regular
any longer? Subject to
change is a sign that
wolves, with their binocular
ability to observe things that haven't
happened yet—e.g., dinner—can read long
before the sheep.

Leaving Town

Not just slung on the son
's back in the rubble of collapse, city and child
unprotected in her studied inattention to
    the chair his
daughters carry
        his moans
the memory of all he was
struck down when all he wanted to
brag her body and the indubiety he had
been inside it only part
of him part her but from him
all he could summon and therein get
the son who would shoulder him
aside from his naked rimes to her
body beyond comprehension but by
daughters to sacrifice as he alone among men had
permit until he was made to limp and still
his unbidden mouth tells her
                      glory only after
death grows close enough to tell instead
the tale of a grander, more degraded world to
come where she is less even
than empire.

Nothing in his life became him as the leaving of it

Office wall blown away first
time at the controls unsimulated world
impossibly below
                    the horizon at
a thousand feet filled with building the room
dissolving in octane fury God watching his moment
to stride out above the witness he banks
who said he wore a red shirt glass rushing
into glass or dive that he might
soar a roar gone black over
the swooning world tiny
voice fading without choice

Further Notes on the Epistemology of Loss

The last supper is of course the one one is
contemned to receive under the house
sauce though it is unclear whether
or not such seasoned her giving in
any conscious way: that she was practicing
up for the city or more that she simply cared to
render herself indelible, that another could
embody lubricity but not that
body in its particulars, course on course.

That he reanimate her curiosity this book then switch
coupling for public celebration, that too calibrated
love inhibits general growth as a longed-for pilgrimage
to the capital is symbol of nothing more than string
tied around a finger long ago lost in a cultural
calamity, the pickle slicer of opinion varied with the breath
of time, its expansions that require the marriage of fresh
fittings that no mate stay long locked lest what passes
through corrode and encrust what was designed for
maintenance of what is inside hence unavailable to those
charged with its custody
that any stimulant propel its object away, its
geometry a progress of loss of power to maintain
the flexibility of what must be rejoined or it cannot
be expected to work, must uncouple or cannot connect.

Kleis who lay beside him
winter nights and summer without

shackles to occasion any
material necessity, without restraint
without doctrinal flaw, with nothing but her

body, her voice, her desire, her
departure then only his future

The return to made wood, only his
warmth at issue
                    at rest on the maul
handle head down seeing in the chips and dust what looks
to be a dessicated tulip
poplar blossom but
there is a string
attached
          one she'd surely tossed
out the window to make room

All the leaves are down into song and the sky
's gray, the house clearly there, its axial truisms
outstanding in the trunken world from the saddle six
hundred feet south and eighty feet closer to the world
's core, a little warm for carrying wood that
distance uphill so he's topless but a vest to keep
the bark off his back.
                          white-phased red
tail quarters above and he freezes, ten foot oak pole
balanced across his shoulders, arms stretched in sup
port of the weight as it circles to check him
out in tighter circles stalling as it passes and flips
back to see him again.
                          They're motionless there for
just that second till it heads toward the next
knob south after a snake drowsing below its den
rock lintel
                  russet tail fanned and flapped
down to brake into
each stall until its turn.

Han Shan

alone
with everything
on it

These days devoted to the chain
that stretches into age's glacial river hand
in hand; the younger on the shore hold
together the one who secures the one who
clutches the one who reaches toward the one
who founders in the numbing flow caught always
before, fought back those eyes of the lost not yet
inured to loss unready for the waters
that move indifferently among us whose momentum
is finally incorrigible the most terrible fate is that
our own minds may rob us of the evening
eddy of care to face the bewildering
blankness of being out of time again
alone. So we seek to make ductile the fibers of
our familiar body that we may steal her back
to us, her eyes once more full of what she got
upon the world and please fate to make more
merciful her immersion in the same river awaits us all.

The Restoration of the Baptist's Daughter

Fall begins as hot but less water
in the air a fitful breeze, the morning
devotions frame the upper window. Sweat
shirt at seven, tee at nine, at
noon, none.
                    Princess won't quit in
want of a lost Kinni
conick, Boudicca of Lewis County camped
across the river and up the criq, the Royal
Engineer attending his instruments of seige that they lay
waste the infidel and recover Kentucky

The Vernal Rise
is in the nature of things, but

don't forget that they shoot
unruly students in this state, and

how much more provocative to Bulldog Hall
when he can't see 'sup; so

taunt whom you must, then turn and run.
Don't give excuses to guys with guns.

Aspirations

Hisai good
    bye husai
'ello
'eronimo to 'uddleston, 'esais
                    "Build a lot
            of 'ouses and leave
        a hwoman in hever-
y hwon."

Somelles

Laura smiling. Elise
wrapping. Angela Smallwood
elsewhere smoking, elsewhere
Angel and CD
too. To
Ron, Donelle

Content fills form
not as water a glass, but
as rain drops
the air, held by
its tensile pressure

Watchcap

the sun
slides
unseen

through
lowery
stratus

behind
the
ridge

leaving
the world
dark

below
washed
above

through
lowery
stratus

the
light
remains

in
parfait
layers

pearl
gray and
various

cream
to milky
orange

behind
the
ridge

in
parfait
layers

the
barge
floating

through
the
etheric

treeline's
painterly
edge

leaving
the world
dark

pearl
gray and
various

through
the
etheric

hori
zontal
twilight

under the
stratus
watchcap

below
washed
above

cream
to milky
orange

treeline's
painterly
edge

under the
stratus
watchcap

of
oncoming
night

Any reply claims
a share
          as the old stiffs must
stalk down the shingle to
strike the whale, theirs by merit
of place among the polity that
ideas are common 'cause
everybody has them
                    that is where
would you carry the prize off
to alone to eat alone warm and light in
the glow of its essential esters
                         with
nobody to talk to or lie
beside to keep
the fire in your sleep

Cardinal defiant late
winter red and mate, her
color blent
with   the hummocky stump they
             stand at the base
             of   an eight inch diameter
                                 black gum butt

he recons one hop at
a time, head swiveled each
step through the leaves
toward   the cleared duff covered
                       with cracked corn
                       there   he perks
                                    a long beat

looking for trouble, she
watches one with
the stump but
for   her red-corn mate-
             eligible beak follows
             behind   always
                           behind him

he concentrates his
scrutiny on his flanks and feeds
she fakes left
and   makes for the corn in
             the corner, he feints
             toward   she flies back
                          behind

he feeds again, she
moves toward the corner
gets in   a few pecks a
             kernel or two
             before   he flies
                          she flees
he follows   her out of   the picture

Impossible to derive the bottom
most point of her either
nether cheek so does
each curve
                out
and up
        in
                every arc

A ringing sometimes audible
to others: the Whistler goes off or on the stove
the kettles adjunct to their hum rise that
much but anymore always in his ear overused behind
guitars horns chainsaws Cats hammer on
plywood. Cold Mountain silence on the ridge no
impediment to her as lives therein between
chimes and hum
                barely there
            the ear
fairly ringing

Retrorogation

Go ahead,   It's true, she said,
Look, he said;   My look's not led

You'll never find   To love so true
A love as kind   And kind as you,

As I.   But I've found one
I'll try,   I love as none

She lightly said,   Other
And went ahead.   Ever.

Either is certainly curtains
                              pure pleasure is only mutual
we have nothing else
from it to fear still
drugs relieve conditions they are unlikely to
eliminate experience can be too much if
it includes nightsweats or bungee jumping off an overpass
onto the freeway at rush hour he could drown in
her negative instance excess would she turn her head
in embarrassment or the vision above her
clutch unbearable?
                              O the bugs, still
heat against which peppermint soap
gallons of lukewarm water over the head
cornstarch loose clothes to wrists and ankles sac
a blossom the decibel level louder than Stuyvesant Town
hylas frogs cicadas crickets the occasional screech
owl whippoorwill chat yellow breast
not the marker at night

Dear Zoomaster

Water on moss is not as slippery that hadn't seen
rain in centuries, a cascade of muscle, that subcutaneous
layer, unfeathered as though she were covered in specie
and couldn't be ridden: no head down tail up in her
program, no spread legs, lordosis. She was cold. Whatever
the medium provided she took as her own, engenrit of
the ardent clutch. Flashing plate, lips round and wide, her
eyes staring in bovine awe, impossible to read, probably
not enough to hang a wedding on. Or a dinner: anything
smaller than herself. She looked at little me peeking
out like it was lunch, those muscled lips all aswallow.
Enough is sometimes too much. Kids aren't in the markers
but the spasms are
like being lifted by the neck and from the waist
down she is a mermaid.
                    The Ostrich

i wanna puke
No, i wanna be here

BUCKET BUCKET T T BUCKET T BUCKET T

Daltry's receding but never ending whine, less
than ten years from Jan and Dean

I WANnit I WANnit I WANnit I WANnit

"If he does not treasure, neither does he cast away the lesser
revelations, saving them one by mean, insufficient one--
some unbidden, some sought and earned, all gathering
in a small pile inside the casket of his hopes, against an
unknown sum, intended to purchase his salvation."
                                        –Pynchon, Mason & Dixon, 408

Compleynte

Listening to you is like watching a ball
game and one guy is telling us what we are
seeing though it is right
in front of us and the other
explains what happened just as tediously but more
so since his pedantry has not the virtue of
effect and the third out is Baby
you're playing both parts.

Moon gone

gibbous on the half foot
plus new fallen
snow
        the luster of
nine pee em, wind
wiping the sky
clear in that
western quarter
                following
back shadows in
footsteps going out

And I had thought the snow
deep going down the curious
angel Tom had slipped in
legible powder to the pick up
                            Mackletree just
passable as far as the lake where Tom is
pulled off in the upper parking lot
                        so I stop
and walk over to where
he is rolling a cigaret and allowing there is nothing
wrong
            he just stopped for the view and I turn to
the puffs blowing sidewise across the ice covered
with fresh snow and almost wish I smoked
in the morning

First blue sky in a while not above
freezing enough to cake the snow down
south through the saddle to the beginning
of the rise to the next knob
                              dead chestnut
oak a long way to carry the dry chocolate
heart and now
from that direction under the filling moon
coyotes sing in the night gone quickly chill

So doth the winter of our discontent give gray laborious
sums of torque.
Windshield shattered and the saw won't run.
Less than a week's worth of wood on the porch.
Cabin kraaled with fallen branches,
The forest wrenched to limbless hulks.
Driveway gone.
The blows continue as fresh snow falls,
but the rest of the world swallows worse:
war, famine, pestilence:
Do not ask the Gods; they have doom to
enforce--that times be interesting.

                    bow saw
                    bow saw
        misery whip

Red oak twenty feet out
the slider over the sink busted
                              its top
dangling parallel to the north wall of the cabin
                                        still
hinged in a twist thirty feet up where it gave
way
        the new top vertical shards like the cathedral of
Gaudi's nightmare
                      the small limbs whose
leukephilic training arched them
                              up now
arcs them down bell choirs of ice
pendant along each inner curve
                              the larger
limbs always at the crown of a confined tree trail
the ground well
                      west of the cabin twined among
the limbs of the neighboring snags that stand
                                        against
the sky stunned
              as the Burghers of Calais

If the gods were going
to make us
                    suffer what we would
need them for what
would we need them
for if
          the question is where
the payoff is there
is where the payoff is
                         look around fresh
snow coats the ground and fallen
limbs surround the cabin
                              still
what
days wood
on the porch and then
what but what
                   the gods provide
plenty
of water or food before
the question ends in
ice the gods
               provide

Solitary grouse stalking through
the snow below the north kitchen slider
crossed her tracks, claws not clearing
the snow
          dragging along, parting the new
and culminating in her clear, three-lobed print
pressed below
on the way to the outhouse, eight in
the morning

Anecdotes of the Late War

1

Ffarewell, the rayn of Crueltie
Though that with payn my Libertie
Dere have I bought, yet shall surete
Conduyt my thought of joyes nede

"Live Karaoke"

Thunder and lightning
Baghdad waits
"Y're damn right i got the blues"
O Goddess
       float
           lightly in
           again
And pound the shit out of me

At the Briefing and the Secretary

                             he says them damn
Fedayeen Terrorists, the nerve to fight without
uniforms just 'cause their daddies didn't
pony up for the Posse de Ville, thereby providing
gratis a gloss on redemptive paramilitaries at least
as far back as the embedded farmers, their shot now
heard at last across the River of Fulfillment
the product of a clearly irregular predicative sequence
involving ricochet and appropriations of torque with
which to spin the globe until the drill
drops into the right hole.
                           Rummy grins
beneath the office windows that reflect all
light above the bridge of his nose back
onto the scribbling fellaheen below
squeezed by the bight he twists into his
story. They clamor for another turn.

Of Course Not. Of Course. You Bet.

                                   I have never
                    says Rummy
              seen any
evidence that the intelligence I received wasn't in
the aggregate acceptable. I expect things to be different
on the ground.
                 On this subject he is
despite some odd non
verbal vocal filler characteristically
clear. The Intelligence did say that
Saddam had dumped his WAD and the Secretary
has made evident his skepticism concerning that
news from the Spooks as he
says On the Ground.

4

The Notorious non
                        pause in the proceedings somewhere
south of Karbala it now appears was inserted
at the climactic moment to allow your local
NPR hook up to roll the logs off its spring
supplication for funds from devotees willing
to pay for the lodging of Eric Westervelt in lieu
of those extra MRE's the grunts outran
                        capital
necessary to replace the taxes of the prospective
pledgers now encumbered by the bailing out of the airlines
to remind us
            all of the difference between
public radio and publicly traded
                        companies. Meanwhile
I'm still wondering who's
embedding poor dear Annie Garrels in Baghdad lost
In the Palestine from which she implores her minders
At All Things
            Vetted By The White House for news from
the Tip of the Spear which
                        by the sound of her
voice she expects to reach her before
the Rockets of Love

5

So are we warned
                    that empires never
last as though stakeholders anxious
to encumber the future of their children
foul the nest in the name of convenience
and endorse a culture
that creates corporations determined to service only
those with shares through surcharging those without might
be chastened by knowing that
the imperial orgy will barely survive the farewell
memorial video Spielberg's atelier was hired to shoot at
further expense to the heritable securities.

6

Nothing more clarifies Rummy's commitment to
the ideal than his insistence
that the story is liberation and any reference to revenge
murder and the plunder of national treasure is beside
the point.
                    But as the guy
who grabbed the reporter's mic
said:
        "The people
veddy, veddy, veddy, veddy
                                tired."
Yet he was free to say so.
                                The question is
not whether he will be free to speak next
year at this time
                    but whose mic will be inclined
in his direction.

7

The yuppies were weaned on the notion that being
born in America gives one the right to grab the brass
ring that swings just within
reach among strobic arrows labeled
                              "opportunity."
But
the children of those fortunate sons were born with
the ring in their mouths
                              and they will never willingly be
without its verdigris taste on
their palates. They expect to live in
the style to which they were made
accustomed
                no matter the cost
to themselves and incidentally
anyone else in competition for the entitlements that bring
that flavor
                not unlike
blood back on the tongue.

But, of course
                     it might be thought that
when the Antiquities Advisory Board
heads told the VeePee Something Needed
To Be Done to save Babylon and Nineveh from being
sacked again
                they were informing the fox
that the chicken ladder had been
left down.
           Not
             so. Il Consigliere had
long before been briefed on the Op to
procure for his new offices inside the mountain under
Camp David prelapsarian golden
oldies. Only the Primary Client had
Mossadim to encourage the curators in separating
The ancient from the ersatz.
                     Just a little
tidying up of the mess liberation
necessarily makes without
line-item expense to the Budget.

9

Soldiers are trained to shoot
when threatened.
                    Asking them
to double as cops is Bad for
Baghdad. Their training, however, would
Actively Affirm them as
first hires for the NYPD.

10

Still now they know
the secret pronunciation
of
    BugDud
GuttT'r
and Mow (somewhere
            between mow
            and mow)
Z'l

Open door hummingbird
hovers overhead before beelining
into the east slider a tiny thump barely
breathing flat in his palm on her belly list
to the right
                Five minutes on his lap in
the doorway shallow breath leathery black
eyelids flutter emerald lashes gray dust
across her breast left foot folded back
                                    Taken in fingers
to check the claw she squeaked pain or alarm and stood
in his palm looked at his face warmed
her wings took off shit and flew to
the upper window where she sits breathing hard then
flies out of sight into the chestnut oak

She was naked but
he was still
in his

                socks: one blue one
                   brown (he had

noticed hours earlier changing
shoes

                meant to correct his
                         error

she chuckled as she looked
down

                 (he was pumping
                       away

past his bouncing
ass

                  "you got two
                    different

socks on"

                 (got another

pair like 'em
in his drawers

                   laughing
                  as she came

What's in an acronym
                    does the job
of naming
novel syndromes
and infections require degrees in both
medicine and advertising
                    not that
we can't trust the public
relators to practice
medicine since the reps have
been replacing hips and prescribing pills for
years
        but do we
really want the doctors getting creative?

Of *Plata o Plomo*

Join or die. The people clearly opt
for competitive hedonism exhibited in
an otherwise aimless internally
combusted orgy of stimulation through
simulation.
                It was Plato first
declared the absolute that is immeasurable
gorge between the good and the necessary but never
has mother been a more unexamined preference
than in the devotions intoned by the young
ethicists waving about their academic credentials, models
of the materially buffed corporate pimp.

The latest anniversary issue of the New Yorker depicts
E.T. in full retro apparently
monocling that pink and green butterfly shaped
like America but observers will note that
young Eustace clearly has his eye across
the spine on the latest Lauren
rep in '80's young Reaganite rig gazing
broodishly back at him. Two fictions
at the service of an indirection.

The Donquis think Ralph might swing
the election again but they needn't
sound the alarum
                    the media are
already altering his prototype from
Quixote to Robespierre, the lost Dauphin's
gore all over his hush puppies.

Sailing from Byzantium

To the death march of the Children's
Crusade the only comparable victims of
recent sacramental groping were those
whose fear of familial shame enforced the silence
no insult could break.
                    More mortally encumbered
were the Shanleyites currently representing the Borgia-
Trungpa faction of the 'Hood which proposes that
priestly acts in the end can never be wrong.
                              Even Yeats
despite the gall that imagined the Irish had gone
out to die inspired by his words betrayed
enough shame to wonder if he'd fucked up.

Like a Rolling Senator

So Tony Tony to
a standing O from the congressional floor
says the poor
               "Americans have never been
more misunderstood" a phantom double
negative Double U might mouth yet
                              "Do as
we will or we will
destroy your country" seems simple
enough to comprehend even the Presidential
diction.
          Blair on
the other hand represents the karaoke of the Angles
his cover of "Sympathy for the Devil" so
weak it cries false the rumour that he is
the get of the aged Mick.
                          Ectually, the P
M graves the imago of Ron Wood: late
hitchee to the wagon of the hegemonic band.

It may be time to review one's total
opposition to the efficacy of capital
punishment
                although fear of death does
not seem to deter child rapists the finality of such
a threat might make leaders who incite
and prosecute unprovoked wars consider just
who at last may grace the list of those that gave
the final measure of devotion to the cause.

A Certain Redundancy
                        There is to
the EU according to Roman
Garanicz, Polish
MP, when prodded
by the BBC gimlet, "No other
alternative" for
Poland. Absolutely
not.

Mute without authority in being
neither husband nor nurse encabined in
the center of oak and tulip forest to
this oak grove extensionless as Lavinia
filia Andronici as anaeolian as her
absent tongue as witness to mutilation without
the mitigation of malicious intent unless
whatever god of the Februa we might admit
assumes the weather dripped ice from the sky
until the limbs no longer tried capacity
to cry was cracked away at
last denied their testimony against October
winds which punish whatever demands
devotion with whatever offers same

All day the lady
beetles crawl the south
wall of the shanty looking
for a place to winter as millions
sacrifice the most exposed
in layers of insulated
death.
      I'm all for all
those bitter little bodies that seal
every inferior entrance
with Greater Stuff than is to be
found at the Imperial Outlet*
                   No
plastic wrap necessary for those
protected by the masses assigned their fate.

----

*Wall Marts

What if we were goats
                    if we were not on
first name terms with the King
of Spectral Decline
                        if we were forced
to address whose robes as intensed
shift below our scrutiny of the dark
recesses the sun survives
                        if frequent
compression did not buoy us beyond
the inevitability of another
declination to caprice

Mom at 86
                    "I feel better when I am asleep."
Standing over then
sitting beside her a little
louder each lowing her
name, her honorific, the distinguished
mother of singers, head
bumpers, who knocks
them off in her
sleep

Cheryl

In the basalt vault all light
delights as though she were, she is
its spring. La Source Levantine. La Gal
Levant in her fancy
                    khaki equals
elapsed time Marseilles Beirut by any
means Detroit Paris.
                    in hand out
on the couch, down in
the throat a purr, agaze along her
stroke. Their hair fanned along
her back, tight as
the waves Jason sailed around
the dolphin trail calyx.
                    the rips in
her heart she allows make capacious more
or less. What we can
depend on will not make us
independent. The rates you raise may
be your own whose cannabinal hum, whose
Io eyes.
            What gives goes. What remains
salves the rent world. Vera Zazulich will
not be here for tea. Another must start
the pipe around and then
the bottle lest all be likewise lost.

Now that beating women into meat is unacceptable so
many men can no longer generate sufficient turgor that
Sildenafil Citrate has plunged deep into the light
truck share of Big Game Minutes available
to flog the product.
                    Just busting all the easy
ass between Jalalabad and al Fallujah hasn't been
enough to raise the flag, but the consideration
that the Undersecretaries of War may have stiffened their
collective resolve by chemical means makes one
wonder if Lincoln would have ordered each of his generals
a barrel
            the effects of liquor and wood on
discretion being according to my father
at least consonant if not congruent and clearly
desirable to anyone who wants a pick up like a rock.

It might prove instructive to compare
the mortality rates of officers
to enlisted men in wars involving
the U.S. How many generals for
instance died in the Civil War as opposed
to enlistees? It would take some
research to discover the answer to that
one but I'll bet you can determine
the exact ratio sustained so
far in our middle-eastern adventure
without recourse to reference materials.

Circling the wagons is what you do when you can
see that you are about to receive a package inside
of which you can only predict is
the ass you've been
unable to locate or look at
the bright side it could be Osama's.

Juncos most
the only things warm
blooded besides the occasional
cardinal or white throat around perch
in the maple and sassafras saplings an amphitheatre
fifteen feet off the porch from which they watch the lead
bull descend in punctilious flits limb to sprout
as he observes one
young and dumb enough to serve as chum hop
out from behind the snow-covered grill
pecking as he goes at
the seed just scattered as they are ready to
depend on what is on whose menu.

The Transubstantiation of Mel

From Mad Max the lovable berserker alone
at last in opposition to the irrationally hostile world
through Braveheart and its sequel to
the rational evil Jesus opposes
                    it is
the rogue cop of the Lethal Weapons
unable to use his powers without
the boss's okay who most mimes
the stricken Xrist
                    though the happy
ending of the latter in which the tormented
misunderstood artist bleeds all
the way to fiduciary heaven is only implied.

That the Boston Archdiocese is decertifying
a hundred parishes and selling off sixty
churches is not saith the pee are father to be
interpreted as retreat

                The Church he avows is just
repositioning itself to face the challenges of
the future

                This is the guy Lee needed to replace
Stonewall

                The Cause was shot anyway though it might
have taken more than a year to yield the fifteen miles
from Chancellorsville to Spotsylvania had Jackson
lived

            On the other hand lost
causes need spinners worse than generals

Who Came First: Six Variations

It doesn't take a chicken
to make a chicken
but it does take a chicken
egg to make a chicken

> Which came first doesn't take
> a chicken to make a chicken egg but
> a chicken egg is required to
> produce a chicken

two non chickens can produce
an egg full of chicken but
a chicken egg is required to get
a chicken which didn't come first

> two non chickens can first
> produce an egg full of chicken genes but
> a chicken egg is required to produce
> the chicken which didn't come first

two non chickens can produce anew
an ova full of genes that produce a chicken but
an egg is required to produce the chicken which
wasn't engineered

> two non chickens can produce anew
> an ova full of genes that get
> a chicken which didn't come
> first but from Perdue

Midnite still beyond
the river at least five miles south across
the twisted ridges a train pulses the tracks, the ground
the air around all the way home on the move up
the creek doe in the road can't decide which
way to go. Stop. Did you ever have to mind your makeup
into drive, scale,
lamp, the pen. Sleep
                    Little
                    Willie John: how I love to
                    pay you back with interest

I Know A Guy

Elder don't
pull no corn until
the water

boils he said
and took a pull on
his BudLite

Sunday evening box turtle scraping out a hole in the chip-thick duff to lay her eggs there for hours, tipped back into her nest. The next morning the area was scuffed up by raccoons, no sign of eggs. After days of rain, started to pull back the tarp covering the lumber stack to give it air, a young copperhead coiled uncovered. Got a five-gallon bucket with small holes drilled in it, placed it next to the stack in front of the snake and used the leaf rake to tumble it off its perch into the bucket and put the lid on tight. Take it up Deadman's hollor; he'll know what to do with it.

Ran a whippoorwill off her nest
two speckled eggs   how did she know which
                                    way I was going
Scared her up again this time
        she flew on   to a fallen branch
                and posed close   enough to see
        her whiskers but
clearly the trailing edge
        of her tail   was red
                    gold

The JAG Officers
                    will counsel the putative enemy
combatants until their dicks run dry   it is all so very
                                very eleemosynary
Last night thighs enough to fill skin
side down a castiron skillet over high
heat doused, i.e., covered with Frank's then onion
garlic, sliced peppers and seasons, the lid and
simmer half an hour before adding chopped whatever
the garden has ready still lidded another
few minutes lid off to reduce the liquid to
goo and serve what doesn't get
eaten the raccoon will relish
smacking her lips
dainty fingers covered with greasy red sauce
leaves a tip, viz, next time
                    save some
meat buddy

Authority resides in the rain
                              that what we call wet
dampens the trees snakes and us without preference
beyond the presentation of surface that may be in some
way penetrated so adhesion establishes molecular
associates without regard to intuition or systematic
understanding whether epoxy or amber resists that natural
coherence, that the agora is everywhere and always
the province of the imagining but no less real for that
which Horace asserts Ulubris contains which claim we can
declare authoritative as rain since nowhere does
everyone know more than elsewhere that the imagination
cannot be verified by doing the same thing again that
there is no same thing that the rain falls in time each drop
coherent in response to surface pressures that inform it as
we are informed by what we can say to others without
regard to position or the definitive qualification of the real.

Io the cow   eyed owl
               imitator stings   when green larva blood
                                         red stripe above inferior
white O but   she always hurts the one
               who touches her

All night the moths fly by
lamplight through the volume at hand then rest
up in the ceiling corners where the hornets
find them for breakfast
                              wings scatter the table

bat passes
through but
the moths are
all too close
to the light

5am Venus out
the window larger than
memory
gibbous over
tulip gnomon east of the garden

The state department
of social services has discovered enough
previously unorganized cash to pay off everybody but
the elderly disabled and indigent who will be
waving good bye from the far side of the river
we just crossed it
is good to be going home

A Song of the Fur

The Janjawiid grow strong just north
of catastrophe on the south side of
ridges they grow
                    tall and potent. They live
to restore the right of the Cavalier to
every virgin.
                    We will uproot them. We will
cut them down their pendant sacs
unspent. We will save intact the flowers
of grace their depredation. We
will immolate them
                    ourselves. May
God bless us that worship
In the fatwa of our astonishment.

Iron on Iron Works

Behind the irons the N&S
tracks and river and across
the river Russell and the CSX tracks and four
lane divided US 23 and then
the ridge.
        North of our table is Ironton low
along the river at the foot of
the ridge US 52 four lane divided and
full.
    At least the air is
moving first breath of an early
fall that won't be much longer.
                           Early
that is. The T in Ironton has lost its upper
mooring and hangs upside down below
the line. The motorcycles carrying Heaven's
Assholes idle awhile.

She Started It

For ten years we cupped our morning
coffee while Bob asked simple questions in
pursuit of the key to our time and as we sipped
resuscitantly Cokie would incant the magic
word
      Look
as though he had something even
simpler distracting him in the sound studio. She did not
admonish him to listen to what she was
promoting since it was standard POV: the insider to
the manner born the Consortrice of lobbyists one
who knows that the bus commands the crown
of the road the expeditious SUVs are no longer
forced to share.
                 But now the Administers every
one urge us to look before they speak—President
to Cab Secs to spokesfolk: the Roves with
their Scotts on Aris—all incapable
of response without the formal marker that declares that
they are planning on saying nothing
demonstrable.
          Look said Cheney
to Leahy and the rest of the sentence
is the subaural message to the rest of us to read
their wagging lips the flag waves in
their lapels.

Turn your radio on

find a vacant stare in pursuit of which we may choose
among watching the administers vomit the slaughter
of the school kids in the Caucasus and the fly-kohled
faces of the infants of Fur or reports of the inundation of
Florida in all of which the god of the Fun
damentally Reborn conspires to protect his own by
effecting the reelection of the Chosen Vehicle

Ground freshly penetrated by the new fallen
dead eighteen months waiting for an event sufficient to set
the recycle scale to rapid
                    the remnant Eye-vun saved for
the Ohio Valley was persuasive to all but the most
recalcitrant continue to hang in
the Damoclean splendor of the bangers on the corner
watching you turn into a dark alley

The Gods do not speak
in metaphor nor do their oracles the great
crime of Oedipus is interpretation one step
ahead of the law reckoning the ruse by which he might
avoid his doom i.e. leave town
                              a sacrifice without
the wit to know the end of humility's absence sliding in
to the queen's bed from which escape is impossible
                              life is lonely
again when only
lush latifah singing stray
horn
          jumping the woodcock
          double yellow
jacket comb scattered about
the hole sound of bird gleaning the leaves frozen to
bring it to sight looked up
                         dry yellow
                         poplar leaf along
                         a sassafras branch
deny nothing don't
want anything

Tony Blair has nothing to say
about the deaths of a hundred
thousand Iraqi non-combatants yet
he "abhors" the execution of
Margaret Hassan which explains his reason for not
offering to trade places with her. Or them.

Moonless not one
clear night a month without
touch, no round, no
light at night.

As the fans go wild
a naked reverse rest
of the way through the woods mackled with
light diminishing in overcast sunset dense
in the horizontal reach across outriding
ridges
        intuitive life gets caught up in long distance
events without relay with only
will to insist the quickest kick is still
to come that precedent pace quicken those
juices remain damp on reflexes alternately
dammed and sluiced by time as adrenal as yards are
striped while the goal is all over the place

Besaddled south agaze humps along
ridges misted with snow
and trees like looking across
a series of montes veneris
                solitude deprived of
human otherworld is my thou perforce
ringed with pearl rose at sunset an hour
later gloaming gone slowly salmon
                    moonshadow
through the latticed sheathing of the uncovered
roof stripes the porch
          last night
coyotes yipped on the next ridge
                glory in
                dischord

Apres Gautier
            when pleasure has broken us
listless between licks we smoke the two of
us taking tea

Fat gray squirrel furry spandex cant mask
the muscles sleek beneath upside down without
effort fixed to a dead red oak stripping bark gleans
larva from its inner surface butt twice wider than his
shoulders

Saved by all that moon rules so far
north as framed in
                    the slider above
the sink freezer burnt porcelain below aural
plate slips through the balance diffuse in ice
fog unreachable but in song
                              in the morning in
the window that crowns the couch roughly
the same distance away
                    that
exile call his own
murmurous moon erect but still
pendant as she is still imagine that
flesh be round desire the pit of him
not reach beyond the window frames another
reflection of what is in
fact behind him
                    that he must be outside
to be in

Body as ground with squishy center the way
back completion of the circuit gone
to town out drowning worms or lost
in the unhouse as usual the way back
worked instantly we were not
you were transported to the celebration you were
looking for the way out switch that
would get it out of you and on the road.
What's a plug without
an outlet a hole without a soul a way
in where difference disappears temp and humidity
static across gaping pores opposed to
somebody to pick up the tab

government might be
used to keep wolves off
sheep but its current
function is to keep regulatory
fleas off wolves

Post-Promethean man declares himself free to make deals with God, but no god gambles with a mortal; what does a man have with which to entice God? Homo Consumptor has nothing to offer but his tiny soul, of which he is obscenely proud but which is useless to God. What would God do with such an item? Gaze fondly at it and murmur, 'That kid gets more like me every day.'

Just to be clear
               There was no
apple involved the fruit was between
her legs the snake in her hand and
what the Master saw that
cool evening as he strolled was her swollen
belly
          progeny is original
          sin that we must
go into
the world to multiply

South slope just off the knob south of the cabin
dead yellow pine top long lost rotted down to less
        than a foot of the ground
the outer fifteen rings remain only on the north side exfoliated
        a couple of inches down and petaled back to mock
        blossom
next thirty still chocolate together though no longer
        integral stepped
        down east and west to duff on the south
core four inches through rises twenty feet to a stub
        supported by a dead black
        gum branch grown opportunely long
        horizontal into the light released by
        the death of the pine
gum gone in turn to the closing oak canopy
every foot or so a whorl of limbs rotted to the fins
        that gnarl longitudinally supporting what's left.
I's a camera.

In the saddle west of the knob south of the cabin just now
a small hound went off flush with something hot
ten seconds later coyotes yipped in the same place
then both together
a yelp then only coyotes
yipping to silence

Spring on the flip flop
                        white-throated
rookie essays the tune but can't get
ol sam peab
                  return
                  like a stuck disc

over & over
the trill is gone

The Terranovans have been accused of being
too dim to invent the wheel but then they did
invent the pipe which clarifies
cultural preference concerning not
only the means but the goal of
transport.
                  Exactly what
percentage of the fun is
getting there depends on where you're bound.

The distribution of wealth
                              A gold coin can
remain at the angle
of repose until some
scion drops it at
baccarat but
                a simpler
way to dislodge
it is
        with a knife

An idle he called himself
fellow as Catullus cited his own
undoing cities have been lost in
downpressor lividity no more than a maroon
ass embossed by the easy
seat Addison and Steele basked in
the opportunities offered by new world coffee and tobacco
their industrious younger brothers shipped
home with the liquid maize to make
a trifecta sufficient to displace the trinity

What Katrina said

The rising tide that lifts
all boats drowns those
without one

Defeat poisons the heart
victory the soul

If you can't learn new tricks you
just lie in the corner and moan until you
can't go out to shit any more and they put you
down

"Of course we have the right to insult God"

The liberty of the glib proclaimed in Le Soir
might well seal the fundamental rump from Colorado
Springs to Qom. The article that faith may be
profitably defended by bullies will stand the last amended
so getting fired is the lesser of the deposed
redactor's problems.
                        One may agree with
what another says while defending the speaker's right
to die for having said it as a gentler response
would mock the gauntlet deployed
to turn aside the Saracen glare.
                        Liberty
allows no bully to carry her flag. One must not
enter the lists without assessing both
the possibility of defeat and the cost of losing
the garden one was advised to tend.

After Seferis
the expression of mind not like oil
from the olive but water through ground
coffee to nourish the necessary that it be not
insipid in the absence of the good

Bebo Valdez meets Bevo Francis
Recuerdo de Habana back
home in Rio Grande, Ojai-
O, it's all in the lip

National flags should reproduce heritage
art: La Grande Jatte would make a great
French flag, Hendrickje Bathing on
the Dutch, one of Hiroshige's views of Fujiyama. We on
the other hand wouldn't have to change much: something
of Johns' maybe, or we could just affix
Warhol's signature to the one we are already using.

Quaternaries

Chestnut   just wandering among the few
auburn   strands that had given
sorrel   up their hue he came
                  to her eyes

primarily
blue rays of
gray there too

Up and down the extension
ladder careless of consequents unwilling to
waste the time to clear the area level
the feet establish the pitch
the strong arm of fate as
always the connection of faith and arrogance.

It's not the expectation that the Gods offer
a laissez-passer but the realization
that nothing else could.

                              time of young things tucked
under the flank mother
presents against the rain
the wind insinuates

Whippoorwill encouchant
                                on the porch roof goes
off five feet from the open window on the other
side of which, the pillow on which, his head:

                                dive and parry
in variation on home the third
audible intake on the uptake, sucking the sack
full to fling over the challenge

Companion chat
yellow breast conspicuous yet
less commanding than the rarely cessant
procession of calls in
indeterminate order any
time night or day

Another oven bird under the window squat
next to stunned he thought to
gather it in his hands offer
a porch seat thereon to recover but
it thought better hopped over his
hand under wing into the under story

a month at last
rain at first vague
taunt the gods swell
a shower for hours
the wrens think
it is over their rasp around
the porch therefromunder towhee
into the hickory then a pair
of warblers out and alert

Going on a hundred but intermittent breezes ease
a few degrees keep the humidity a little
better than Eden were Eve in

Hypothesis and proof notwithstanding the truth
emerges in the commerce of actual events
and can be spied only in relation to the particular which
is what the muses told
Hesiod: that among the lies the true
thing appears by chemical reaction as a gas
and a metal make salt as salts make certain
concentrations into the impulse that reaches the lips.

The Lateral Undulation of A. Hatchet

*The sea piles against
the inflorescent mountain.
The wax my bees make
contains tiny grains of salt*

Oxalis yclept
sorrel fm ME sorel fm OF surele fm OGer sur meaning
sour as in
sourwood aka
sorrel-tree so called for its bark is
sorrel an umbery orange
            sprays of tiny white
          cups panicled midstory in
          'a sea of green's
sour as oxalis in salads and
sourwood bees their favored honey as one
           tree equals a clovered meadow or
           a glade full of the oxalis commonly
           called common wood

sorrel

At the neighbor's to talk shop work, who'd seen, that morning, a snake sticking its head up out of a hole in the tarp that covered the woodpile and had shot it, thereby explaining the clap as of two planks smacked together he'd earlier heard. He went out to the woodpile and took the tarp off. The snake was halfway up, bridging two tight four-square stacks: a glossy, dark-phased young timber rattler—four rattles to a button, it turned out—watching them, a raw spot where the slug had torn away the skin from the top of its head. He picked up a six-foot sticker and fooled with the snake until its head was clear of obstructions and the neighbor shot it again. It slumped, maroon blood dripping from its head. He poked it out of the stack. It slid off the stick and began to swim away. He picked it up with the stick and carried it over to a stump and laid it across the top. It rolled off, heading for the woods, but it was doomed, so he whacked it at the base of the skull. The stick broke in half, but the snake stopped moving. He carried it home to the cabin, nailed it through the anal pore to a black gum and slit it from the anus down the belly to the ruined head. He slit the tail back past the scent glands, cut the skin free from the anus to the end of the slit in the tail, sliced the snake in two behind the glands, and began pulling the body toward him, using the knife to cape the skin, first from the belly on both sides of the ventral incision, then working around to the back. When he got to the mangled head, he cut it off, leaving it, along with the tail and its rattles, attached to the skin. The long tube of meat was unshadowed white, seemingly without sinew, one sinuous muscle attached everywhere to the skeleton. It could have been succulent over mesquite, but he threw it to the coons. The hide was delicate as a lady's chain mail, velvet scales in wide bands of chocolate gold and ochre, lapped over silk spandex skin. He laid it out, scales down, on the grill cover, an old enameled steel table top, and buried it in kosher salt, traife nonetheless, though the coons couldn't care. Clear weather would desiccate it in a few days. Cleaned, emolliated, worked, saved against the ritual slaughter of the serpent, that the dangerous world may be declared perverse at our convenience.

Kneeling on the east roof of the new
print shop to side the clerestory while the bumblebees work
the sourwood a few feet north of the shop wherefrom they will
repair to the grill top near the cabin porch to
pinch a little sal de machado for their wax.

Greñudos Hediondos
                              skinks & swifts
more often heard than
angle away from the tremble of Jovian
steps down the path into the crawlspace
between duff and brush

Animals sparse at the end
of a dry summer - just so much
water on the ridge still
impounded in the ruts Tom packed in
the clay through which his driveway crosses the otherwise
inscrutable top of Horner Branch. It keeps three deer slaked
but no squirrels when the nuts are poor only
vagrant raccoons leave
tracks in the mud around the faltering
potholes still deep enough to cover the odd frog.

The perfect expression of Capitalism is cosmetic
surgery. Who with a million bucks worth
of debt wants to try to recoup by treating the ill
the lame and the halt whose conditions are linked
reliably to their inferior game plan.
                                    The rich
may be in fact sick as dogs – though not so poorly
as the uninsured - but
you'd never know it by looking at them.

Tight quarters demand the unhandled be
put away but it's the indeterminate
rotation gets stowed
things lost to clever cover
                            the candy tin in
which years of paraphernalia collected
bunched canned and left for head
scratched frustration when it comes
not to hand as meant to be
employed some other day

boxes of books of
no immediate referential necessity

Vanity at sixty inhibits
development of what is there
to hope for that is
not a product of caring about what's beyond
the desire to excite others on sight despite first impressions
incur interest on an unredeemable principle

                                        your assets
are considerable but no citation of them suffices
without occurrence they lost the cherry ripe somewhere
between Campion and Herrick the Bard informed all
concerning what her eyes were not since
denial appreciates in forms no spaniel at heel could
conceive
           conceit
conceals nothing intimate as a fart for anyone
worth knowing that gas makes the skin glow even
a Bugatti is more beautiful when it is moving the mask
a barrier between lips and eyes we see out of
be looked into and hair then to
touch and taste and know no visual arrest each inch of
which retards not the development of desire but
the desired development

Why should a woman not smell
                        like herself perhaps
refreshed but absent
masks of any variety rather than
a compound not excluding whale vomit concocted to
the imperial taste of one hyper-olfactory decider

A Measure

        That time after it gets too
dark to read yet while there is light
enough to fill the lamp trim the wick and polish
the chimney is sufficiently slack to
attest the slick fit of just that
interval into the day

West along the crest
                zero
through the snow bright sky walking up
on a deer bed packed translucent snow still
damp with abandonment
               her purchased
warmth lost to the dilettante trolling blinded
by clarity into her boudoir

               small doe scared up ten feet on the bank
she takes a few steps and freezes enormous ears
open toward the interruption hoarfrost
lengthening her muzzle so she looks like a long-legged fox
only the outline of her body the same umber and dun
of the duff litter winter saplings surround her

That palm is never the seventh
sunday the one that steps off
the cliff in full assurance that what he has come to
do however partial however a line
there lived on despite the forgotten
mission as well as those codicils designed to elaborate
specifications in order
to elaborate duties he has
been given to know are vouched safe to the fool

The spring displacement of the brush inside
the tree line enough for several
hundred feet of pale to keep
the young peppers and beans out
of deer inwards has by early May given
way to a retreat inevitable as any
expeditionary force exiting Russia or taking
the longer view the Fertile Crescent already raspberry
canes lean out from incumbent forest to
take back the day by August paths
to the outhouse, garden, berry patch, truck.

Whippoorwills in trio
                         sets up lapping
frequencies resolve into chords as they drift in
and out of phase
                         hanging skillets from the outer porch
stringer to drip when one went off three feet
overhead on the porch roof modulated into a subsident
insistent call: a low "pa-pa-pa-pa-pa…" in rapid monotone
slowly
decaying to pianissimo
                         pocket flashlight played
along the rafters unsure of the source then
into the yard
                         the beam spotted two
scattered overhead wheeling above
the woodpile around the east side of the cabin
white unders catching every photo-
reflective residue of the day

The nearest NPR outlet just switched to 24 hour xmas
music not a burden instead of going to sleep
to the BeeB overnite I listen to the ringing in
my ears and pretend it's crickets chats
the raccoon sorting the garbage the occasional
train ten miles down the creek across
the river in Kentucky when the wind is
right by midsummer frogs and toads
crickets and cicadas would drown
out even Lucy Calloway in Adams County
where the new programme caps the 150 year shift
from the party of Lincoln to the base of Bush

Dark continuous call of the screech
owl child struggle to hold sleep
windpipe strung with snot
rattle and whistle at once

Name the only thing
that separates swifts of fence from those of post so
sure they are of superior reflex squatting
to scrutinize a skirt of sloughed skin
a regenerating tail jury rigged to a shoulder
stump the finger inching through air just
touching till the other crosses
the green zone gone

Two wood frogs in the west
rut of the twotrack to Tom's: she's open-
palm size flat; he's not much
more than half that, still riding, equally
squashed: like the song
says: truck comin'only
one got brakes

The paraphernalia of belonging
                              loads
every titanium frame wheeling the gentle
sag—six hundred feet in ninety miles—down
the west bank of the nutrisour Scioto
and up the Ohio the scenic route along
the flood wall cum million dollar murals
to the Civil War Memorial in the park where
they can buy the same brats and bud—across
the street of course from K.Rogers—that they'd get
a hundred miles north while identifying
the natives as those not in bright whatever
came after spandex emblazoned
with names conspicuously not rendered
in English a bright day to be
anywhere: eighty degrees sun easterly
breeze to keep the water in
the river rendering unnecessary the technical outfits
as they coulda done it in chinos and a tee shirt

RIP

The bearer of bad
tidings is dead now
all news will be
good no more friends
die rivers ride easily
within their banks water
clear in cupped
palms and the cars
of chargers run
lean to the checkered flag

Chat calls without regard for invitation or
challenge a pleasure consequent to command
of the crown no crow's nest these: sun
breeze the absence of what might
bring down his boxcar repertoire the pull
chord at the base of eggshell skull   chips
whirs   warbles   whistles   trills
croaks   random without scale beyond Homeric
tropes fire unconsidered as snake eyes make it new no
pressure to trip the gate dams the flood

The Blogger of the Dogged Slog
just thought
he'd mention it, thought most
weren't at attention, guessed
there wasn't much to say, still
pages later, tailing the Nantucket
sleighride of the idea, lost
in the ozone notion

Money is spongy enough
to comfort if not satisfy
the greedy or bananas of
which there is always another
crop
        Time's commonplace
that one
has all there is
notwithstanding we can absorb no
additional stores thereof

Cleaning the press when
the dope chopper pops over
the ridge from the north low
and fast past the shop the cabin followed
by a set of interlocking loops of the clear
cuts to the south first
coil around the closest show brought it
almost over the ridge into the garden before
it broke back concentricities growing
faint as it spiraled south another
independent contractor practicing for Baghdad

Dappled Things
                    Doe and two
fawns in spots watch from
the pool where Indian Camp falls in
to Upper Twin behind one short
of a murder rises black
flags iris into mackled light

A Sign Lady
eclipses only at full
      moon holding in
      horns the tidal rise
                please
haven't I returned with you each time
      exhausted on the margin
      of the dark children
      waving goodbye
              turned back
into the woods – past it – silvertip
      looking down through leaves
      into the run – tired of killing to live – of
      fighting for the power to produce
              O Lady
let me live to live – let me work – allow me
the strength – the words to make
the song will console them in their sorrow
              What good to
grow
old if we cannot ease others with
      the appropriated meat of our experience – the
eclipsed
      moons of our love – full and occluded
      by need for the other of commensurate
      if immeasurable weight spread thin so as not to
break
into light through light through umbra lost

In late light gray squirrels are cutting
nutsack twigs out of the red
oak top to drop eighty feet a rim
shot against the tin roof just over
his head inside a tom tom
                              lyric
conjugates third that squirrel that
tree that roof essential to the shot – not
narrator but character – a tell
the story told as the curfew does
the knell of parting day

New moon through the trees bloody in
a dry world wherein the only
refreshment you carry as you come
uphill fighting for air unwilling
to rest before all that succors the parched

The cabin enpalmed wherefrom
spatulate paths finger the world: one to
the neighbor, the shop; another downhill
to family and commerce; the rest into the woods.
Within Beltiste hand held fingers running
your ridges release those fragrances that preserve us

The muses themselves point out that amid the true
things they say are some number of things untrue even
the price for admitting their need to follow words through
the world of fits the hand of
sensation quicker than the reasonable eye

It's a question of idiom under the heading
ass, perfect a photo of her curled
naked on the couch while under
perfect ass a picture of him at
the desk next to her, writing it down.

When Hera first laid brother Zeus Homer says
Mount Gargaran [tickle] sprouted a carpet
wildflowers to buoy them as her fundament rocks
above the crush of ginger and daffodil
that rose between her
trap undissipated absent
volition and only so full

Fraught with daughters their
worries their despair their unruly
children whose eyes shine with inclusion
that lights likewise the weight of
the load all these constraints on
the freedom they have not
learned to conserve so
certain of it have they been

Proust allowed that
living is like walking on
stilts that gain an inch each
year: the clearer the prospect the more
stumblesome however love constrains
these stilts as it extends the view

The Runway

fall quarter the ballers were
wearing Carhartt bibs with one
strap dangling winter
quarter the post-xmas counselors are easing their junk in
the same way next
year sure as shit the campus will look
like hiring hall at the carpenter's union

                    The world at 32
degrees of limb ice rimed
while the drip line beneath
the eaves patters susurrant
cymbal ride plus cross time rain barrel
plops that catch the pattern

Two Etudes for Mike

An ascent
in tone from the first
to second in a series of
two signifies assent though
descent asserts dissent so
thumb echoes voice

A measure
she six steps to
his quarter note foot
retread a bar to beat
daddy six to

Vernal Signs

Augie Barker, 36 years gone

Flu taking hold the fever
introduces a delirium that twists
the transmission to that focus at which perception is
refreshed and slips quickly
on leaving the road to the contagious
hospital in the deep woods first ocherous
hints of red and yellow in the crowns descending
the hollor below the small rain driven
diagonal past the window against the long smoke-
gray vertical oaks siding the opposing slope

Elpenor's son sink bloodlessly lower as spring
carries each year your poem north on the phoebe's back

She's here who is the moon no less
summoned as last summer invoked then
praise first the one that heard that plea
that fidelity win voice september ripe fresh again
among fruit pie of the morning cellared yellow
delicious and cherry orchard pick a preserve of red
raspberry and jalapeno together in the garden
that is the present

חאנא

The name given
Louis' mother was *Chana*
                              Just that
tongue roll under the alveolar ridge
that drawing together of the chords
gives voice to the sound that makes it
yours yet
               who that heard Louis say
her name could find another
absent the glottal rattle that turned
the head of the first grace

The hard man rides ever on
falling water pursues that
which pulls him turns
aside if pushed that he be
not at the mercy of currents

Dale: a valley (o.E. *dael*)
Hollow: a small valley (from o.E. *holh*)
Glen: a small, secluded valley (Gaelic *gleann*)
Dingle: a small, wooded valley (M.E. *dingle*)
Dell: a small, secluded, wooded valley (o.E. *dell*)

So what was the farmer doing there?

Love is a process
of matching perversions   So what
                    Was the farmer
                 Doing there?

Mallarmé: Poetry should make air
                 and silence hang around
                 a word

                         or a farmer

Some Translations of Amen

You bet that's
an affirmative let's hope
so objections to the contrary
notwithstanding just do
it soitanly I can
dig it 'tis
a consummation devoutly to be
wished bingo that
hound'll hunt you
go copacetic by pressing
the # key, I confirm
my agreement right
on absofuckinlutely

Zoe's roof on Bear saves
another pops one or two seventy five
minutes in the dentist's chair thornless
blackberries huge juicy insipid prone to
monstrosity easy to pick gallons a day juiced to enjam any
day wallpaper eyelids at night glossy uniform hung in
bunches organize the light of passage tomorrow shingles
unchanging person behind the eyes all these
years it's the same few teeth demand
squeaky wheel status everything changes everything
but the eyes looking out clarify
the twins absolute separation identified
in my daughter's womb distinct
sets of eyes index icons as soon as they see

Post-erectile Bexley a wreck he steers between
the new plantation that shades nothing yet
shows somebody thinks trees will be
available in twenty years. Somebody won't
walk under them. All the combinations are in
the popper doubling down by the minute grows
necessity as preference is put in place wherefrom it is
constrained to blow smoke up the hostess' ass splendid as
she thinks it beats with her heart that is close to the same
size but susceptible to adrenaline dump her private
party with invitations tendered only by the former
organ says the bar is down until the number comes up
and the long walk to Picnic Point begins again

'

Against the strain and solitude of exile
the hound and lash of service
she became whore and saint to his design
the cunt and comfort of home

O Io your
comprehensive
tongue that it bear this weight

"As Long As You Are Here, I Expect You To"

All closed in wiring traced and sorted the run
around the room begun drops tacked up every
four feet or so pause to pick a spider off
her dress and cup it to the deck no solitude but at her
whim that muse may as easily dam
the words as compel them

As soon as the roof is on place
appears sacrosanct a nail to hang
the tool belt: hammer tape speed square set
slick scribe fasteners at hand.
                              Extension coiled
above saws: circular jig reciprocal. A shelf to hold
journal pen herbal consultants bevel gauge.
                                        Rafter

square hand saw level suspended
offcuts stacked sacked or sac'd

Steps and stair
cases flip the rafter square in complements
along the horses rise and run around a constant
inversion wider treads demand
a gradual ascent the way the Spanish
steps are not a ladder and the ponder approach to
the seat of Lincoln would never get a short redhead inside
the eye at the top of Washington's other obelisk

New bed loft geometry
tucked against the ceiling rake looks
out the northwest slider screen dark but
for the unseen light facing the church of free-will deflected
white frame hovered six inches west in the sight
field maybe twenty degrees of arc of yellow
vapor haze around the bulb above
what remains of Setty's Service since folks
now get gas and groceries in town but not
religion yet another function of location cubed

Touch bases the ground
where touch is ground as intransitive
flex in the way that *she feels good* does
not describe the skill she touches
the ground with but the proprioceptive rise
to the rushes that flush her or else
his voice reflects transit of predicate ground

All things bewildered wonders if gov't-financed
experiments – in Panama of course – mean that
we should consider cutting down the forests
to conserve water

                  a question that moves the public
discourse one step deeper into the mystic
science that finished Weimar

October almost gone in
spectral rise in task heaped on the vanity
of problems solved anent the problem
that never dissolves matter if not the corrosive
nature of desire for the full wood
shed a griff on the hook the one in whose
eyes labor is praise and never enough

Spinoza sought to comprehend the form through which
value may be replicably measured and thereby understood rather
than count on the particulars in their profuse
idiosyncrasy uncertainty revealed
the vanity of any such refusal to acknowledge
the centrality of event of the hearth that
a thousand acres of trees holds at its center a silence
frequent beyond scrutiny an absorption of harmonics that
renders understanding cellular and ubiquitous

Party of the Dead

alone in the woods how tell them
from the deer but by diet
and of course   mixed dancing

twenty five years but my father is
alive to my senses even
now I know what he feels
like his odor his voice each of his steps
the dance he knew

To the line
To the lane
Puts it up
Puts it in

Dull chain ai ah

But the monster
drops it does not

barberchair land on
the dogwood just below the x roll
down slope nor hold
either soggy sapwood
or heartwood rot

An excess d'estime
were there any

to estimate a good
six weeks of wood step sidling the slope up to
the cabin the woodyard
the stack the porch the stove

The upward way determined
not by length but maximum
gradient and the character of obstacles between
that which needs transported from the spot
it occupies and the destination presumed for it.

Solstice

For S.

Deposit
Deposed
Disposed

Again to the lake five miles there
and back again to the lake five miles
there and back again to the lake
five miles there and back
again in her deposed

Turkeys in the pine tops

Last of this year's Mohicans spent
the longest night with her sleep hand
at rest cops the other insinuates the nether
twins comprehended cornsilk Mohawk
fleece in heavenly peace

He quarters down the south face toward the split rounds, scanning the woods for straight—or curved just so—sour gum saplings for handles: two to three inches through over four feet, unbranched, dead a year—though green sticks can cure in the porch rafters. The longer dead are rotten in the manner of gums. The living wood frets and frays but cured fibers lock around each other so there is no grain along which the wood may split. He once drove a splitting wedge plumb through a sour gum round sixteen inches long and not much wider than the wedge. He thought it was white oak until the wedge was three quarters buried without radial effect to the gum, after which the problem was retrieval.

"*I dare, Madame, I dare.*" Unlike Cezanne, the focus is often weak and shifty, susceptible to distraction. But daring crosses hairs, planets and words align, some conjunction of discretions coalesces into some arcade of syllables that has no other excuse to exist but that we wander along its lines shopping for what we didn't know we needed.

In the saddle at the end of day's light
reflected everywhere a white world clearcut
background overlayed with sapling strokes cadmium
milked from the tube against what washed
grays steady the eye drift pearly ceiling
beyond the lines of ridge constant
shatter ice-fat twigs hitting the crust all through
the woods behind a distillation of silence
challenging the eyes' ability to record

Snow now in crusted
layers of strong almost enough to hold
weight giving in snowshoe webs stuttered
crunch loud enough to turn a buck's ear on
the facing slope path clear fifty yards into
compliant oaks opening sunset into pockets of blue

Eight inches of snow then froze and four
more of powder to a second cap difficult through crust
saplings bound everywhere to the ground the mainline in
the cove open to entry not without
alarm the deer nested there body heat
invested in dry beds reluctant unable to
browse does belly deep through the crust

The panicled drupes of the staghorn scale
vermillion scarlet through crimson appear
maroon to the glance but all hues
dull even Friday enclosed in lucent
ice doubled their size and bent trunks
to the ground they were without
luster
            Saturday morning well below freezing open
sky first time in a week everything cased in
ice against snow but the panicles were free
and brilliant melt-wet reds surrounded
by white
            Today still clear breezes forty degrees
warmer than the world melting panicles
gone flat and chromatically mute again

Last night those first warm winds shook
the ice from the limbs each tree letting go
at once as the first branch to unload swung
back up and jarred the whole tree free so
the entire load like ice cubes tipped from
a dump truck on the edge of a forty-foot cliff at the bottom
of which the cabin roof four feet above the pillow

Hammerhead yammers scallops
air among oaks
                lands
cocks an ear for larva
scarlet flash against the snow

Never lonely again among daughters
never again lonely among daughters never
lonely again among daughters never
again lonely among daughters never lonely
again among daughters never again
lonely among daughters never lonely again
among daughters never again lonely
among daughters never lonely again among
daughters never again lonely among
daughters

Driest march in memory i.e. ours no
vernal appropriations to mark the change though DST saves
what energy time derives from squaring the light clicks in
the brains of whose credits depend on the measure
that commodifies the stream in which potency is
turned to revenue without losing its juicy essence

In what sense might the trees be said
to respect the other apart from as part of
the appropriation of as much of the commons as they can
support though the light remains above all
reach for it limited by capacity to pump against the grave
earth's pull called depressive for refusing governance by
will even expressed along the horizontal highways are
shared with a comity that respects the irrevocable but
avoids appropriating the path of the other in order
that the first-part party be not reapportioned as well might
words be guided with similar restraint in light
of the Pyrrhic outcomes common to boundary disputes

Indulgence

No word more misconstrued than that
sweetness the Pope copped to offer those who could
pay for their proscribed pleasures with no more
than temporary discomfort marketed currently
as the surrender one affords only one's own hope
to find the right reason for doing a wrong thing

Jonah

The signs are ordinarily confusing enough to offer
doubt concerning which course would
provide passage but when
instructions from God are delivered
personally the relevant query is how quick
He wants one to be about
the task it would be
a mercy to give Mom a reassuring kiss goodbye

Sleep Studies

Drawing her draws on the relief of
features two-day stubble mounting her
mound piñon spaced on a mesa from
which washes the narrow draw Rodin was
drawn to intimate in its definitive crease

But now she is off her
back onto her right leg left over
parallel to its mate the length of
her thigh away as perspective presents
bilateral glutes like the flying sea
gull a subscript brace embodies shadowed
crack breaking into light above the lost
coccyx curves up the spine to infinity
balanced on her other
shoulder chestnut waves along the pillow

Traps cleaned
utility panel replaced
pressure valve ditto
protecting the lie minus intractable human
corrosion clogged lumps that cannot be
renewed replenished or rendered capacious yet
must be handled to wear smooth their edges through
daily abrasion by touch and its sustenant oils

Having a woman—of course one can
not if she has herself but access to same is at issue constant
as what rain compels and as intermittent for which one
grateful is not drowned in the different
effects limited by survival on the one hand and death on
the other whereas she although one
of her kind affects the desire to abide such rain or no
kind of rain has parts that can be stroked with light so
their contours make the fingers ache like a throatful of
chocolate neck and shoulders
breast belly and thighs' sweet choke—is
a condition skin tight in the rain

Walking the creek bed he picked up a siltstone fragment nickel-sized but shaped like Ohio on the map. Further down a weathered hexagonal bath tile about three inches across the points. They rubbed together in his pocket until changing jeans he laid them on the writing desk. The next time its surface needed cleaned they got tossed into a brass ashtray among projectile points, potsherds and like curiosities. Mending something weeks later he noticed the two pieces, dotted the center of the tile with left-over two-part epoxy and pressed the stone to it, which assemblage stuck around for thirty-five years, coming into focus every so often out of whatever clutter it had held subliminally in order. Then he pinned it to the kitchen wall with a pair of roofing nails, its most conspicuous venue in ages of being shaped so long before Ohio was.

The privilege of necessity
again the hiatus of love the choke
point of creation bent work abandoned in
thanks for the instances love and a full notebook provide

Cat crouch   redux
                        sprung back to sense
the sensory dispensation   flight
of the deserter   escape
of the prisoner too many said
JRRT confuse the two   it is not in
his world a matter of
perspective orders the monk
abandoned the heart knows it is
the difference between post and cell comrade
and keeper lip and lock the one
that hums the one that bites

Summers' brush surround
the cabin cut back against indian
summer fire from below bent to boot
tops clip sassafras and maple saplings creepers
grapevines bound around bramble and briar tugged
stacks dragged and tossed onto the garden
kraal amid rampant growth not
a sign of chordate life
                        birds in the distance call for
a minute or two GE rumbles prototype
engines twenty miles by the 4pm due-north crow

Just over the knob west of the cabin two new
buck scrapes urine scent strong ten
yards away even to diminished
human olfactory receptivity fresh doe
prints deep as she was
compelled to squat
                        antler musk and oestral
pee turn
back and let them be at it

Standing on
                        A forty foot red oak log thirty inches in
diameter at the butt unable to roll
the rest of the drop to the run as it is
wedged upside of mature though thinner
oaks at either end
                        facing down hill
arc of piss rains on
a colony of dried-up puffballs yellow cloud of spores
rising like Chaplin's gulls fly backwards
out of the sunrise most of the day's clarity
turned it into quarter rounds – saw maul
wedge axe – followed by silence not a bird
flits the seed rich thickets nor sunbathes in the oak tops no
message from time's quiver reversed by the human need to
fuck with things
                        chopping away
rotten sapwood packed with grubs which
messengers in time might better use

Firewood trail just north of parallel to the ridge late
afternoon solstice sun winks over the brow
peripheral to my right eye with each step a glance
left across the hollow displays a shadow
crown bobbing through the tree tops light
the heart at her smile's flash

The local sandstone base is rusty tan layered
by geologic with a fine grit dark
chocolate when fractured layers sometimes
relieve glyphs to tug at the limbic vale of making yet
no distinction between emotion and thought as glandular
ache of the ages that brought us to this
capacity to imagine the actual in what was
old stone long before it cracked a nut

Tuning
        the woodpile runs straight down slope
its tallest point against the skinny red maple
that keeps the stack from tumbling toward the gap
two hundred feet below
                        the topmost piece
seven feet from the ground
high as the splits can be comfortably lifted
the other end
twenty feet uphill toward the shack
only three
        the ground
uneven ages of unmoldered duff
chestnut splits irregular
ridgetop wind broadsides the pile
resettling the pieces
                 every few days
the sticks tapped plumb with the maul
ring in the cold
           each at its own pitch

If it's not working out
for one it's not working
out for any
        cottage sucked
empty by fear unrelenting
the bell dogs jar God's
vermin all night caged
hounds against
the fence bounce in their
shit where
        power is
to the people by kilowatt hour by
rechargeable toy phone teevee
apiece by fans of fridge attic
ceiling air exchange full of
static as though friends were
a distraction family all that
mediates the gaze lovers
chase around the pot Keats
portrayed
        likeminded bodies' longing
minds at odds not working out as bodies longer

Last Waltz for S.

Larva rappelling out of the chestnut oak
suspended eye level for a little
interphyletic information swap though it's hard
to imagine what this dangler might be
learning from an unsuitable target or worse
a dancing partner too big to dip whether
the descendent completes—his need-to-know
payoff—the pupal close or simply awaits her wings

The venerable dogwood above the old
skid track twenty yards downslope
north of the cabin has heeled over
the cut bank below

               its top at rest
spans the track kept otherwise free
of woody growth to stop fire burning
up hill

       it's stable there—no rootwad
exposed—twenty degrees past horizontal canted
enough to escape at last being
shaded by the tall oaks that cup the cabin

Leaves still
green on strangled stems
shrunk so for the first time
since may the moon is shapely
through the oaks though
still not halfway
up her ecliptic highness

Fragment 55

You'll be dead forever unremembered
undesired denied even one
Pierian rose invisible as
your companions in Oblivion erased
blown away with
the rest
        nobody knows
who you is but Sappho
wanted to hurt her for
a long time the poem survives
as ready invective just pass it
on you will never rest

He's Hera's in resident attachment
the world all those versions of her demanding
coins & bulls & lightning—three months his
sack full of Baby God she was not
supposed to notice—thanks to twice-
cursed Teiresias tattled her nine times
as much fun as has the big guy as
though he sought sanction to trot out the droit
de seigneur and explore the best
fresh legs in the Xoros
                         The balance—no
Europa, no Thebes—allows the tenants to
think rationally about the ways
the daughters of Nyx keep kicking
their asses around
                         It's not owed to any
lack of uxorial come on that
master strays but all the more / reason to write in
her honor as long as she accepts only what
then cannot fail in hopes that she will
take her ninefold pleasure there

Boar black bear gone gray around
the muzzle nested back on his right haunch
left leg behind head he licks his balls in
the dark mist of thighs thick against his
of seasons past of threats claw scored higher
up the trunk or to take not the charge
but to the brush therein to groom
his own moon below the looming ridge
one day beyond full before him horizon a glow
behind his back the west goes blind

A Finding

Guillaume de Poitiers:

Farai chansoneta nueva
Ans que vent ni gel ni plueva

The band of clarity
that separates fronts stretches all
along the latitude even on watch
tower ground horizon open

time to turn with

the shadows trees stir
descant to the omens the ever
later hour warps through
the ever fresher breeze

will work new verse
in front of wind & frost & rain

We're actually a lot
alike fellow laborers but one
came with the odd operator's
manual on no hand special simply
not unlike the Great Gleason as
R. Kramden au table at the restaurant
with Alice Trixie and Norton in lieu
of dessert the latter three order each
in tongue demitasse but Ralph demurs
weary of ritzy cuisine and calls for instead
a small cup of black coffee at which
faux pas the audience titters however it is
they whose certain feet step in the wrong anyway
that's what it says in the OM citing
the American idiot with a foot
variable as the difference between what dampens
culottes consequent to the first tongue
kiss and the subsequent cocktail slipped
from the cup petite but profound
enough to fulfill its craving for the foreign
as proof of the depth to which it may contain the other

Also Available from **UNOPRESS**:

William Christenberry: Art & Family by J. Richard Gruber (2000)

The El Cholo Feeling Passes by Fredrick Barton (2003)

A House Divided by Fredrick Barton (2003)

Coming Out the Door for the Ninth Ward edited by Rachel Breunlin,
    The Neighborhood Story Project series (2006)

The Change Cycle Handbook by Will Lannes (2008)

*Cornerstones: Celebrating the Everyday Monuments & Gathering
    Places of New Orleans* edited by Rachel Breunlin, The
    Neighborhood Story Project series (2008)

A Gallery of Ghosts by John Gery (2008)

Hearing Your Story: Songs of History and Life for Sand Roses by Nabile Farès
    translated by Peter Thompson, The Engaged Writers Series (2008)

The Imagist Poem: Modern Poetry in Miniature edited by William
    Pratt, The Ezra Pound Center for Literature series (2008)

The Katrina Papers: A Journal of Trauma and Recovery by Jerry
    W. Ward, Jr., The Engaged Writers Series (2008)

*On Higher Ground: The University of New Orleans at
    Fifty* by Dr. Robert Dupont (2008)

Us Four Plus Four: Eight Russian Poets Conversing
    translated by Don Mager (2008)

Voices Rising: Stories from the Katrina Narrative Project
    edited by Rebeca Antoine (2008)

Gravestones (Lápidas) by Antonio Gamoneda, translated by
    Donald Wellman, The Engaged Writers Series (2009)

*The House of Dance and Feathers: A Museum by Ronald W.
    Lewis* by Rachel Breunlin & Ronald W. Lewis, The
    Neighborhood Story Project series (2009)

I hope it's not over, and good-by: Selected Poems of Everette Maddox
    by Everette Maddox, edited by Ralph Adamo (2009)

*Portraits: Photographs in New Orleans 1998-
    2009* by Jonathan Traviesa (2009)

Theoretical Killings: Essays & Accidents by Steven Church (2009)

*Voices Rising II: More Stories from the Katrina Narrative
    Project* edited by Rebeca Antoine (2010)

*Rowing to Sweden: Essays on Faith, Love, Politics, and
    Movies* by Fredrick Barton (2010)

Dogs in My Life: The New Orleans Photographs
    of John Tibule Mendes (2010)

Understanding the Music Business: A Comprehensive View edited
    by Harmon Greenblatt & Irwin Steinberg (2010)

The Fox's Window by Naoko Awa, translated by Toshiya Kamei (2010)

A Passenger from the West by Nabile Farès, translated by Peter
    Thompson, The Engaged Writers Series (2010)
The Schüssel Era in Austria: Contemporary Austrian Studies, Volume
    18 edited by Günter Bischof & Fritz Plasser (2010)
The Gravedigger by Rob Magnuson Smith (2010)
Everybody Knows What Time It Is by Reginald Martin (2010)
When the Water Came: Evacuees of Hurricane Katrina by Cynthia
    Hogue & Rebecca Ross, The Engaged Writers Series (2010)
Aunt Alice Vs. Bob Marley by Kareem Kennedy, The
    Neighborhood Story Project series (2010)
Houses of Beauty: From Englishtown to the Seventh Ward by Susan
    Henry, The Neighborhood Story Project series (2010)
Signed, The President by Kenneth Phillips, The
    Neighborhood Story Project series (2010)
Beyond the Bricks by Daron Crawford & Pernell Russell,
    The Neighborhood Story Project series (2010)
Green Fields: Crime, Punishment, & a Boyhood Between by Bob
    Cowser, Jr., The Engaged Writers Series (2010)
New Orleans: The Underground Guide by Michael Patrick
    Welch & Alison Fensterstock (2010)
Writer in Residence: Memoir of a Literary Translater by Mark Spitzer (2010)
Open Correspondence: An Epistolary Dialogue by Abdelkébir Khatibi and
    Rita El Khayat, translated by Safoi Babana-Hampton, Valérie
    K. Orlando, Mary Vogl, The Engaged Writers Series (2010)
Black Santa by Jamie Bernstein (2010)
*From Empire to Republic: Post-World-War-I Austria:
    Contemporary Austrian Studies*, Volume 19 edited by
    Günter Bischof, Fritz Plasser and Peter Berger (2010)
Vegetal Sex (O Sexo Vegetal) by Sergio Medeiros, translated by
    Raymond L.Bianchi, The Engaged Writers Series (2010)
Dream-Crowned (Traumgekrönt) by Rainer Maria
    Rilke, translated by Lorne Mook (2010)
Wounded Days (Los Días Heridos) by Leticia Luna, translated by
    Toshiya Kamei, The Engaged Writers Series (2010)
Beyond the Islands by Alicia Yánez Cossio, translated by Amalia Gladhart
The Garden Path: The Miseducation of a City by Andre M. Perry
Together by Julius Chingono and John Eppel. The Engaged Writers Series
The Combination by Ashley Nelson, Contemporary Poety Series